ACCOUNTING FOR DECISION MAKING:

A Study Guide

ACCOUNTING FOR DECISION MAKING:

A Study Guide

Melanie Hicks

SYNERGISTICS
Raleigh, North Carolina 27615

ISBN 13: 978-1-934748-07-7

Published by Synergistics Inc.,
Raleigh, NC 27615
info@synpub.com
First Edition: April 2010

Printed in the United States of America
14 13 12 11 10   1 2 3 4 5

FORWARD

When asked to write this Forward, I was reminded of the following Native American legend.

An old Cherokee is teaching his grandson about life.

"A fight is going on inside me," he said to the boy. "It is a terrible fight and it is between two wolves. One is evil - he is anger, envy, sorrow, regret, greed, arrogance, self-pity, guilt, resentment, inferiority, lies, false pride, superiority, and ego." He continued, "The other is good - he is joy, peace, love, hope, serenity, humility, kindness, benevolence, empathy, generosity, truth, compassion, and faith. The same fight is going on inside you - and inside every other person, too."

The grandson thought about it for a minute and then asked his grandfather, "Which wolf will win?"

The old Cherokee simply replied, "The one you feed."

You may be wondering at this point in time how the legend is relevant to *Accounting for Decision Making*. It is a matter of attitude. An attitude is a habit of thought, based on our values and beliefs. These values and beliefs are, as seen in the legend of the two wolves, "the ones you feed."

When I ask most folks what they think about when they hear the term "accounting concepts," I often hear responses such as: "it's boring," "I can't understand it," "I am not good at math," "I am a leader, not a number cruncher," "I had to take Accounting in college but am glad it is over," and so forth. At the same time, when I ask these same folks what they believe to be the universal language of business, the overwhelming response is "accounting."

It is easy to see the beliefs underlying such attitudes. The basis for such beliefs is a fundamental lack of understanding of the true value of studying accounting concepts: to make effective and quality decisions in business. If they had this fundamental understanding, they would see that using accounting information greatly enhances personal and organizational effectiveness, including overall quality of professional life within such organizations.

If up to this point you have been "feeding the wolf" that leads to lack of understanding regarding the enormous value of accounting concepts as decision making tools, I can say without reservation that as you begin to "feed the other wolf," your attitude toward business decision making and success will change.

If you are "on the hunt" for success in any field or walk of life and have not yet acquired it, then perhaps you have been looking in the wrong places (or feeding the wrong wolf). Over the last 30 years as a professor, consultant, and entrepreneur, I have taught thousands of graduates students and travelled the world interacting with many diverse cultures. These experiences have taught me that there are in general two clear reasons why people are not successful at what they are attempting to do. Successful people tend to believe that a reverent and respectful attitude towards the Lord is the beginning of all understanding and they focus on feeding the good wolf.

To be successful in your business endeavors, a fluency in accounting concepts is essential. You will need to begin with the Biblical mandate that fear of the Lord is the beginning of all understanding and be prepared to use the language of business to help make high quality decisions. This book is designed to help you in your journey to gain both universal elements of success.

Brian Satterlee, Ed.D., D.B.A
March 13, 2010

CONTENTS

MODULE 1

Chapters 1 & 2

Module 1: Chapters 1 & 2

Cost Management Concepts

When one thinks of cost management, the first thought may turn to the ideas and concepts of accounting. While accounting is the language of business, accounting is not about the numbers; it is much bigger than that. The underlying concepts in cost management, deal with what a manager does with those numbers, and what they actually mean. Specifically, how managers can use the information to develop, implement, and change the company's business strategy to one that is more successful than the previous strategy.

Various authors will attempt to list and define the actual stages through which the information needed for a company's success is formulated. At each stage, the functions of accounting and how the information will relay into strategic decisions is essential. Obviously, those making decisions must have the information necessary to make those decisions, and the higher up the corporate hierarchy one goes, the less detailed the information becomes. Thus, upper management sees primarily a macro-view of the organization. It is from this vantage point, however, that some of the most important decisions are made. Consequently, accurate and timely information is essential, which may mean that the clear delineation of the stages is blurred.

Various management techniques, such as the balanced scorecard, value chain management, benchmarking, total quality management, theory of constraints, etc., have been developed as strategy tools to assist management in maximizing their potential, and fully utilizing their resources, in an effort to make the company more profitable. As a result, management chooses those areas within their corporate culture that will aid in making their overall business strategy a success.

Strategy

In business terms, how successful one becomes ultimately lies in the formation and execution of a well designed competitive strategy. The problem is that there is not one set competitive strategy that will work for every company. Further, the formation and execution may go according to plan, but those that have been in the business world can tell you that this is not always enough. When things do go according to plan, the tendency companies have, when they are market leaders, is that of complacency. Thus, each company must be diligent, and in a constant state of evaluation and adjustment, in order to avoid the various pitfalls that may befall a company's leadership team, and consequently the company.

One way to combat complacency is through the identification and analysis of a company's critical success factors. Most basic management texts discuss the need of a SWOT (strengths, weaknesses, opportunities, and threats) analysis. While this is a good start, conducting a SWOT analysis does not mean that analyzing these factors will ensure the success of one's company. Again, it is what is done with the information that has been gathered that is important.

Therefore, it would actually be better to create a SWOT matrix. In a SWOT matrix, the items that are utilized for the various components should be those that are measurable. These measurables will then easily tie to a company's critical success factors and the balanced scorecard (BSC). When defining those items that are measurable, they should also be ones of value, as ultimately these items relate to the financial statements of a company. Consequently, the SWOT matrix will become the foundation from which the company's strategic plan is developed.

For example, suppose a company identifies those items that it feels are critical to the future success of the company (i.e. critical success factors). If the company does nothing to measure these areas, or does nothing to improve those areas that need improving, then not much has been gained by the simple identification of the critical success factor (CSF). Consequently, management must analyze the CSFs on a continual basis. As previously stated, accounting is not just about the numbers. As a result, management utilizes the CSFs to create those areas that are most important to the success of the company through the use of a balanced scorecard (BSC). The BSC is then utilized to measure and evaluate the progress the company has in meeting the CSF. The act of measuring and evaluating should be a continual process, as the company strives to become the industry leader. When done properly, the BSC will allow management to see where they are, how they got there, and determine the steps to get to where they want to go. Management may find that a strategic change in their plan is necessary. That is okay, as long as those changes are not done in an irrational manner. Even changes need to be well thought out, even if done in a quick manner. Time is sometimes of the essence, but one should not jump from one ill-conceived plan, to one that is destined for failure.

Biblical Perspective

The key concept in the first module is that of proper planning. The Bible is replete of examples where planning was conducted prior to execution; whether those plans were for good or for evil, whether successfully implemented or a disastrous failure. The same may be applied to the business world. No matter what plan of action a company takes, there is nothing new (Ecclesiastes 1:9). History certainly repeats itself, though it may be manifested in different ways. Thus, company executives must be thoughtful and deliberate in their actions; taking care to examine all aspects of a plan, even if that means having contingency plans, or looking at what the competition is doing or has done in the past (Proverbs 16:9).

In the business world, as in life, this translates to the fact that no matter what type of planning we do, God is ultimately in control, and whatever He desires to allow to have happen, will. This does not mean that we should sit back, and not use our God-given talents for His glory. Rather, we are also commanded to do everything for His glory, to show the world that we are his sons and daughters (2 Peter 1:10–11).

In the business world, this is not always easy. Actually, it can be quite tough. In such a carnal world, doing the right thing is not always the most popular or sought after virtue. Yet, companies that have attempted to implement these virtues have succeeded (e.g. Southwest Airlines), and have done so quite effectively.

The use of management tools, such as the BSC, is a way for companies to examine themselves. Just as Christians should examine their own life, and seek repentance for their sins, companies should examine their strategic plans, and make appropriate changes based on strategically sound business sense. While proper planning, execution, and examination will not ensure success, it does allow the business manager the ability to be as fully prepared as possible.

Application

The story of Gideon defeating the Midianites (Judges 6 and 7) is one that defies logic and common sense. How 300 men could defeat an entire army seems impossible, at best. Yet, as is often the case, God takes impossible circumstances and makes them possible. While this is not something that we, in our humanity can do, God can, if we allow Him to use us.

How can the use of management techniques, such as the BSC, allow managers to turn seemingly impossible circumstances into possible ones?

_____

_____

_____

_____

_____

_____

_____

If there is nothing new under the sun (Ecclesiastes 1:9), then how can the management of a company implement "new" ideas successfully?

_____

_____

_____

_____

_____

_____

_____

Critical success factors (CSFs) are used to measure those items that a company's management has determined to be vital for their success. These factors may have a financial, customer oriented, internal business processes, or a learning and growth perspective. While they may be difficult to follow, there are numerous biblical passages that instruct us how to live and be successful in God's eyes (e.g. Joshua 1:7-8; I Chronicles 22:13; Ecclesiastes; to name a few). Can biblical principles be applied to a company's successful implementation of CSFs, and if so how?

_____

_____

_____

_____

_____

_____

_____

_____

NOTES

NOTES

MODULE

2

Chapters 3 & 5

Module 2: Chapters 3 & 5

Cost Management Concepts

Cost concepts are often left to the accountant to figure out; however, managers should be aware of the different concepts, and how it affects their bottom line. For example, using traditional costing techniques, while easier to calculate, and therefore less expensive, is not always the appropriate method to use. There are times when, because overhead is based on a predetermined overhead rate, utilizing the traditional cost method may actually understate your expenses. Depending on the product, the overall contribution margin could be significantly lower, and could actually be negative. Obviously, a negative contribution margin is something that a company would try to avoid (there are exceptions, but more on that later). Thus, the accountant, and the manager should examine the different methods available to them, and choose the method that is most cost effective and appropriate.

Types of Costs

All costs may be classified into a type of cost. The three main types are variable, fixed, and mixed costs. It is important for the manager to know the type of cost any given expense is, as it will allow the manager a better understanding of how to account and adjust the cost, if possible, as well as budget from year to year. For example, if there is a fixed cost, such as rent, which can be modified by moving to a smaller warehouse; this is something that the manager must consider. The move may not be feasible, and just because it is cheaper does not always mean that it is something that should be done. Again, the manager must decide, based on all available information, as to what the appropriate decision is.

ABC Costing

ABC costing is one method that is commonly utilized in companies today. It is often more difficult to calculate, and as a result, is also a more expensive process. The important thing to remember about ABC costing is that if one is going to implement this form of costing system, it is best to ensure that it is done correctly from the start. The person doing the implementation and/or groundwork must also be familiar with the operations of the company, in order to know how to properly classify costs, as well as the proper allocation of those costs into cost pools.

Once the cost pools have been identified, the manager and/or accountant (usually the accountant) must also determine the resource costs, the cost objects, and the cost drivers. All of these items work together to allow the accountant to determine the true cost of a product. The cost of the product is what management needs in order to properly set the sales price, and to determine the contribution margin, also known as gross margin, for the product. Ideally, the manager will set the sales price such that the sales price covers not only the actual product cost, but also covers portions of the general and administrative costs, which include items such as overhead. It is these indirect fixed expenses that can cause a manager to lose profits, if they do not properly plan. Once the prices are determined, then the necessary sales volume may be derived to determine breakeven and profitability.

Traditional Costing

As mentioned previously, traditional costing is more frequently utilized, particularly by smaller companies, and is generally less expensive to calculate. The key concept to glean from traditional costing is that it allows managers an opportunity to relatively quickly determine the cost of a product. Managers must be able to get information, particularly information related to cost, in a timely and efficient manner. This means that the information must be easily accessible, and must be accurate. If it is not, the manager has the potential to make poor decisions, which in turn could cost the company a significant amount of money.

As with the ABC costing method, costs are broken down into various categories with the purpose of determining the actual cost of the product. Once the actual cost of the product is known, the manager may work with those in the sales department to determine the optimal price to sell the product. Keep in mind that the higher the price of the product, the more likely sales will decline. Therefore it is extremely important to determine what the market will bear in terms of both price and supply (i.e. supply and demand).

Inventory

While determining the price of inventory can be difficult depending on the method being utilized, there are also other factors that must be considered. For those companies that are merchandisers, inventory is essentially calculated at cost, and recorded into one account. Companies that manufacture their own product, however, find that it is not that simple. Inventory is broken down into three main categories: raw materials, work in process (also known as goods in process), and finished goods. It is these three accounts that now make up inventory, and all three must be managed properly in order to keep the flow of goods from experiencing bottlenecks (i.e. the Theory of Constraints), back orders, and other delays. Further, for manufacturing companies, inventory is a vital component in the budgeting process, as the sales budget and the purchasing budget are interrelated.

Calculating Inventory Costs

In a manufacturing company, one would start with the raw material purchases. Any new purchases would be debited into this account, thereby increasing the raw materials account. As the material is used in the production of the product, the account is credited, and in essence transferred to the work in process (WIP) account. Just as the direct materials are transferred, the same is true for labor. Those who are actually directly involved in the manufacturing of the product (e.g. assembly line worker) are considered direct labor, and their wages are transferred into the WIP account. This provides the cost of the inventory that is now in process. There is still more work to be done, whether it be adding additional labor or materials, in order for the product to be ready for sale. Once the product is ready for sale, the amount of the product is transferred out of WIP by a credit to that account, and into the finished goods account through a debit. When the item is sold, the costs are then transferred out of the finished goods account and into the cost of goods sold (COGS) account. It is important to remember that those items that are indirectly attributable to the cost of the manufacturing of the product will also need to be accounted for, and is done so in the WIP account.

While accountants will typically do the calculations for this process, managers must understand the need for each of these accounts to be accurate, as well as the amounts going into the account originally. Further, it is with these costs, that the accountants develop a cost of goods manufactured statement, which will specifically tell the manager how much it cost the company to manufacture the amount of inventory. To calculate cost of goods manufactured (COGM), all one needs to do is add direct materials used, direct labor, and factory overhead. In contrast, COGS includes COGM, by adding COGM to beginning finished goods and subtracting ending finished goods. Both however are utilized in the determination of net income. Manipulation of COGM or COGS will directly impact net income. Thus, the manager must understand how these items are interrelated in order to properly manager earnings.

Understanding formulas in words can sometimes be confusing. Therefore, the following shows in a pictorial manner how to calculate COGM and COGS. These formulas can then be utilized by managers to further analyze where managers can save costs. Ideally, the production department should run lean, so as not to run too much in overhead costs (e.g. inventory storage). There is a fine balance, however, as one does not want to run too short on inventory either.

Beginning Raw Materials
<u>+ Purchases</u>
Raw Materials Available
<u>-Ending Raw Materials</u>
Raw Materials Used

Raw Materials Used
+ Direct Labor
<u>+ Factory Overhead (includes all indirect items)</u>
Cost of Goods Manufactured

Beginning Finished Goods
<u>+ Cost of Goods Manufactured</u>
Goods Available for Sale
<u>-Ending Finished Goods</u>
Cost of Goods Sold

Value Added

Measuring and calculating the cost of a product is necessary. It can sometimes be an arduous task; however, it is one that is essential for any company that has inventory. Most companies do not have the luxury of being monopolistic. Rather, competition is fierce, which continually drives managers to find new ways to cut costs. Fortunately, companies that are on the higher end of the price spectrum can still survive. The key is to add value added activities. These activities set the company apart from the competition.

Value added activities can be as simple as remembering a customer's favorite drink (e.g. Starbucks), to more complicated activities such as custom orders in a quicker turn-around time (e.g. Dell Computers). Whatever the activity is, managers must find a way to capitalize upon it, as doing so will enable them to gain a competitive advantage.

Application

Numerous examples of properly managing one's costs may be found in the Bible. It is amazing to ponder how much detail went into measuring the quantity and cost of items, all without the use of computers and other technological advances that are so relevant in today's world. Examine the story of the building of the temple in I Kings 6 and I Kings 7. Notice the great detail that went into the building of the temple. Now examine your own life. Do you take this much care and detail with your own personal budget? What about the resources given to you by your employer?

Now consider the parable of the landowner and the vineyard workers in Matthew 20. Not everyone was paid the same hourly rate. The same is true in today's time, as different workers will be paid different rates; sometimes for the same job.

In both examples, it seems as though the "owners" did not worry about the cost. For example, with the temple, Solomon built the temple to the Lord's specifications, and God provided the funds. With regard to the landowner, the landowner paid each person what he thought was fair, even though it was more than what was actually expected. How do these two views differ from what the world would say?

_____

_____

_____

_____

_____

_____

_____

The primary goal of most businesses is to make a profit. Now consider the parable of the ten talents in Luke 19:11-27. Obviously, most managers would like to be able to have 10 talents and double them; however not all managers have this ability. Managers have to work with what they have, which could be net losses. Therefore, how should a manager go about making larger profits that honors God? Specifically, think about your labor force, vendors/suppliers, and customers.

_____

_____

_____

_____

_____

_____

_____

_____

The Bible directs us to do everything to God's glory (I Corinthians 10:31). Therefore, should we not be offering the best products possible? How can value-added activities allow us the opportunity to do this? When one considers value added activities, what types of activities should a manager be looking at?

_____

_____

_____

_____

_____

_____

_____

_____

NOTES

MODULE

3

Module 3: Chapters 10 & 16

Budgets

Most individuals will prepare a personal budget at some point in their life. Doing so, allows individuals to account for future revenues and expenses; thereby preparing their finances. Ideally, the budget allows for those unexpected expenditures that always seem to arise, as well as ensuring that there is also money set aside for savings and future growth.

The same holds true for businesses. Budgets must be created in order to ensure the resources of the company are spent or saved wisely. The budget provides a roadmap for the operations of a company. While there may be an occasional detour, the overall plan should be followed. Please note that there are exceptions; however, those exceptions will hopefully be rare.

There are several different types of budgets, but any budget should begin with those who are closest to operations. This bottom-up approach not only allows lower-level managers and employees an opportunity to feel like they have directly contributed to the success of the firm, but it makes the most sense. For example, if the shareholders wanted sales to increase by 10%, but the sales force new this was impossible, then why set the budget up for failure. Similarly, if the sales force new that it could increase sales by 10%, then submitting a budget for only a 5% increase, simply to look good when you brought in more sales than what the budget called for, is also not wise. Not only will executives know you underestimated your budget, but there could be dire consequences. Since most managers have year-end bonuses based on how well they meet their budget, this is an area that is wrought with potential deception. A good manager should have made good hires, and can therefore be reasonably certain of his team's capability in meeting goals, without having to over or under budget anything.

The first budget that should be prepared is that of the sales budget. Without the sales budget, nothing else can be prepared properly. Remember, that this should be as close to accurate as possible. In other words, one should not plan for a 5% growth rate, when 10% is more likely. The sales budget is the necessary first step for both the manufacturer and the retailer, because knowing the amount of sales will help to plan how much inventory is required to meet the demand. Thus, the production or purchases budget would be the next budget that should be prepared.

The production or purchases budget is the second budget that should be prepared, as the company has to have the inventory in order for the sales to occur. If the inventory is not there, the consumer will go to a competitor. The calculations are relatively easy; however, it does take experience to know how much is needed. For example, if one were to start with zero inventory at the beginning of each month, and it took one week to get any product ready for sale, then this would mean that no sales could occur within the first week of every month. A company would either lose sales, or there would be a backlog of product. Since this is not the proper way to a run a business, most managers will attempt to estimate the amount of inventory needed on hand at the beginning of the month in order to meet the beginning of the month demand. It takes experience to get the amount accurate, or close to accurate. The amount is usually expressed as a percentage of the next month's sales. Again, once the percentage is determined, the calculations are fairly easy to make. Consider the following example:

A company desires to have 20% of next month's sales on hand at the end of the current month. If the company estimates next month's sales to be 225,000 units, then the company should have at least 45,000 units (225,000 * 20%) on hand at the end of the current month.

While all of the budgets are important, the most important thing in a business is cash flow. Therefore, the cash budget is one of those budgets that is also essential to get correct. Knowing when one's receipts will come in, versus what will be paid out, allows the manager to adjust buying and other spending habits, as well as the tightening or loosening of accounts receivable standards, even borrowing in order to obtain additional cash, or the repayment of loans. The proper management of the company's cash can help sustain a company going through a rough economic time. If the cash flow is not managed correctly, a good company could fail.

Flexibility and Analysis

Budgets are not exact, no matter how hard one may try to get it that way. Therefore, it is essential that the manager review the various budgets for revision on a periodic basis. For some companies, this could be on a weekly or daily basis. Most companies, however, will review budgets on a monthly, quarterly, and/or yearly basis depending on the entity, the industry, the competition, and the economy. Further, managers should be certain that when comparing the results of what has actually happened to that of the budget, the two should be comparable. For instance a budget of 10,000 units sold is not comparable to actual sales of 12,000 units. The budget must be flexible and adjusted to show what should have happened at the 12,000 unit level.

The easiest way to adjust budgets to any given level of activity is to first break down the sales and the variable costs on a per unit basis. This per unit amount can then be multiplied by any level of activity that is desired. Thus, the flexible budget is a much more useful tool than a standard static budget. Once completed, the flexible budget may then be compared to the actual results.

Comparing the actual results to one's budget is always a good idea, as failure to do so, indicates that a budget was never needed in the first place. In contrast, examining the differences between the actual results and the budgeted amounts allows a manager to review where improvements can be made. This analysis is done through the calculation of variances. As a company purchases certain materials, a standard price should begin to evolve. In essence, one could expect to pay a certain average price. The same would hold true for labor rates, overhead, time, and quantities. Once the standard amounts are known, this will aid the manager in knowing if too much time or money is being spent in comparison to what the average prices should be.

In addition, once the variances are known, the manager must determine if those variances are favorable or unfavorable. Favorable variances are of course desirable; however, there are times when one part of the calculations will be unfavorable, still resulting in an overall favorable position. This merely means that management then knows what area must be improved upon.

An easy way to remember how to calculate variances, and whether those variances are favorable or unfavorable, is as follows:

Actual * Actual   compared to   Actual * Standard   compared to   Standard * Standard

If the number on the left, as a result of the calculation, is larger, then the result is a favorable variance. Conversely, if the number on the right, as a result of the calculation, is larger, then there is an unfavorable variance. The two variances are then compared to determine the overall variance. For example, assume the actual cost of a product was $10 with a standard cost of $8. The actual amount of material was 10,000 board feet, and the standard number of board feet was 12,000 board feet. The calculations would be as follows:

$10 x 10,000 board feet	$10 x 11,000 board feet	$8 x 11,000 board feet
100,000	110,000	88,000
10,000 F		22,000U
	12,000U	

Since the 100,000 is smaller than the 110,000, then this indicates that less board feet were used in comparison to the standard, which in turn causes a favorable quantity variance (i.e. the number on the right is greater). In contrast, the 110,000 is greater than the 88,000, which indicates an unfavorable price variance. The overall variance is then calculated as 12,000 unfavorable.

The results of analyzing the variances allow managers the opportunity to revise prices and manage costs; thereby ensuring that there is a continuous process of improvement in the budgeting activities. Keeping the budgets up to date, and as accurate as possible, will allow the manager to compare one period to another, make strategic decisions regarding pricing issues, make decisions with regard to sales mix, and adjust operations as needed. Failure to have properly functioning budgets could cause a company to be less productive and efficient in comparison to the company's competition. Thus, budgets may be used as a tool to remain or become the industry leader.

Application

Budgeting is essentially the proper planning of one's resources, including time. Failure to plan properly can have disastrous results, in both one's professional life, as well as one's personal life. When discussing budgeting, it is important to note that the emphasis is on planning, and planning well. There is an obvious difference in the end result, when proper planning versus a poor or nonexistent plan, has been utilized.

For example, in Luke 14:28-30, Jesus warned those that were following Him that there was a significant cost in doing so. Specifically, Jesus was warning those that thought the journey might be easy that in fact, it was going to cost them quite a bit and they should evaluate those costs first. The same holds true for businesses that are planning how they want to operate. All of the costs must be analyzed and compared to what will be received. If one purposefully over budgets then not only has the budgeting process become useless and meaningless, much like salt that loses its saltiness (Luke 14:34-35), but there is not a true depiction of what is likely to occur.

Assume you have been placed in charge of the budgeting process. From what you can tell, some of the managers have inflated their expenses to gain a bigger budget. When asked, these same managers claim that they do not know how much the costs will be and that it is better to be over budget on costs as opposed to not planning enough and falling short. Using the passage mentioned above, as well as others, would you agree or disagree with this philosophy? Explain.

_____

_____

_____

_____

_____

_____

_____

_____

Assume you are in charge of calculating variances, and you find that your labor costs are too high. By cutting a few of those who have been with the company a long time, and are therefore paid a bit more, the labor variance will turn significantly favorable. Those who are paid more; however, are the more experienced workforce, and are able to ensure a higher quality of product is produced. If you are faced with cutting the labor costs, what would you do?

_____

_____

_____

_____

_____

_____

_____

NOTES

MODULE

4

Module 4: Chapter 7

Introduction

In this module the reader is presented with some practical application concerning costs and how those costs should be allocated. Often times, particularly in manufacturing type industries, there are costs that have accumulated as a result of a particular process. The resulting costs however benefit more than one specific product. It therefore becomes necessary to allocate those costs among all of the products that are produced. Unfortunately, this allocation may not always be an easy thing to accomplish.

Cost Allocation

As mentioned previously, it is sometimes necessary to allocate shared costs between products and/or services. This may occur in a job costing system or a process costing system. The direct costs tend to be the easiest to determine. In textbooks, this is often given in the problem. Therefore, the focus will lean towards the allocation of the indirect costs. Depending on the information given in the problem, essentially what one should do, after allocating the direct costs, is to look at how the indirect costs were derived. For example, if the indirect costs were related to production, then one could assume that an allocation should be based off of machine hours. If the costs are related to labor, then it can become a bit more complicated due to the potential that Department A services Department B, but Department B sometimes services Department A.

Therefore using the direct method, one would take 100% and subtract the amount of time that Department A services Department B. This will provide the base for Department A. Next, take the time spent working for the production Department C and divide by the total just calculated. Do the same for Department D. Of course, actual examples can be viewed as complicated; however, if one goes through the steps not only would it hopefully become clearer, but one can then see how costs can easily flow between various departments within a company. Many companies have several departments; whereas, other companies may only have one. If the company is a production company, then the likelihood of having to do these types of calculations are much greater, as the likelihood of having several departments increases. The key is to make sure that everything gets allocated, and is done so in a fair, equitable manner, that represents to the best of its ability, what the true allocation should be.

MODULE

4

Joint Costs

Another major concept to be discussed is joint costs. Joint costs are those costs which have been incurred for more than one product. A good example of this would be a cow. There are a lot of costs that go into the raising of a cow, and there are a lot of things the cow could become (e.g. hamburger, steaks, etc.). For instance, if the cow was going to be divided into hamburger meat and filets, there are several factors to consider. If one were to allocate the costs of raising the cow based off of weight, then there is a larger percentage would need to be allocated to the hamburger, as there is more hamburger meat than filets. If, however, the costs were to be allocated based on resale value then more of those costs could be allocated to the filets, as filets sell for more. Whichever method is chosen, it is important to read the material given in the problem, as it will specify which way the costs are to be allocated.

Application

While there is not a lot of material covered in this module, the material is important. If costs are not allocated properly, then the result could have disastrous effects on the income statement. It is possible to actually be selling an item for less than its cost, which is something that most managers would not want to do.

Think about the building of the temple during Solomon's time. Solomon was one of the wealthiest men to have lived, yet he was also one of the wisest. While "money was no object" when it came to the building of the temple, there was still an accounting for the materials and labor that were used, as those in charge would be held accountable. One could not cut corners as exact materials and specifications had to be used. Now think about some of the items that went into building the temple. Could any of those items be considered joint costs; meaning, the materials used benefited more than one item? If so, explain which items and how they are joint costs.

_____

_____

_____

_____

_____

_____

Now think about the redeeming work of Jesus Christ. It is His death on the cross and the physical resurrection that has allowed for the atoning of sins. Remember, God required a blood sacrifice to atone for sins, even in Genesis with Adam and Eve; God had to kill an animal to provide them with their new clothing. Consequently, only someone who lived a perfect life, as Jesus had, could be that perfect blood sacrifice, and do something so gracious and merciful. Yet, anyone who came before or after Jesus was not perfect, and had or will have a multitude of sins. Christ's sacrificial love for each person has paid the debt that would be owed for each believer's sin. God does not evaluate sin on degrees of levels, with the exception of the blasphemy of the Holy Spirit; rather, sin is sin. Therefore, imagine the shared benefits of Christ's death, among all believers, who realize and accept how much debt has been paid. Could the benefit received versus the death owed be quantifiable? If so, how? If not, why?

_____

_____

_____

_____

_____

_____

_____

_____

NOTES

MODULE

5

Chapters 8 & 9

Module 5: Chapters 8 & 9

Introduction

Determining the costs that have occurred in the past is a relatively simple, but sometimes daunting task. The simplicity is due primarily to the fact that the costs have been incurred. Allocating them appropriately becomes the difficult part, particularly for the indirect costs. Incorrectly appropriating indirect costs or other overhead items can significantly impact the financial statements for the negative. Allocating them appropriately however can provide the manger with the opportunity for better planning and the potential reduction of exorbitant costs. Thus, this form of cost control has the potential for allowing a manager to predict future costs; thereby making the budgeting process that much more accurate and useful to the manager and eventually top management, and the investor.

Hi-Low Method

One of the easiest ways to estimate costs is through the Hi-Low method. This method essentially allows an average of the variable costs, as fixed costs remain constant within a relevant range. To actually calculate the Hi-Low method, one first takes the highest sales price and subtracts the lowest sales price. This figure then becomes the numerator. One then takes the difference between the high price of the cost driver minus the low price of the cost driver selected. This figure becomes the denominator. One then take the numerator divided by the denominator to arrive at the variable cost per cost driver. This figure then allows the manager to determine at any given sales level, what the variable cost per that cost driver will be. This is of benefit because since the fixed costs remain the same within the relevant range, one can determine what the breakeven point is for that same given range. Consequently, managers are then able to forecast expected costs based on a given level of sales, which is essential in the budgeting process described earlier.

Other Methods

There are other methods that are also available, such as regression analysis; however, these methods are beyond the scope of this text, particularly as computers will run the regression analysis at the click of a button. One should be familiar with the concepts, but again, the actual calculations are primarily done with computers.

Cost-Volume-Profit Analysis

Cost-volume-profit analysis (CVP) is another tool that is utilized by managers on an extensive basis. CVP is something that, when used correctly, can provide valuable information to a manager. In order to utilize this tool; however, one must first understand some of the terminology, which is often discussed in undergraduate accounting or finance courses.

Contribution margin (CM) is sales minus variable costs. It is this figure that allows managers to calculate items, such as breakeven. The CM may be calculated on a per unit basis or on a total basis. When broken down to a per unit basis, the CM may easily be calculated for any given level of activity by multiplying the CM times the number of units sold. Essentially, the manager needs to know how many units need to be sold in order to breakeven. Once this is known, then anything sold over this amount will be profit, within the relevant range.

Breakeven may then be calculated in units or dollar amounts. To calculate the breakeven in units, one must first determine the CM per unit. Taking the fixed costs, divide the fixed costs by the CM per unit. This will result in the number of units per month that are needed to be sold in order to breakeven. Each unit sold above this number will result in additional income, and therefore additional profit. Keep in mind that this is all within a relevant range. Essentially what this means is that your costs are only going to be constant up to a certain activity level. Once your costs reach that certain level, they will increase; whether it is the variable cost per unit, or the overall fixed costs. The reason is that as production volume increases, eventually, there are additional costs that must be added (e.g. repair and maintenance).

Calculating the breakeven point in dollars is relatively easy, particularly if the number of units has already been calculated. If the number of breakeven units is known, then one would take the number of units, and multiply it by the sales dollar per unit. If it is not known, then one must first calculate the contribution margin ratio. To calculate the contribution margin ratio, one needs to take the sales minus the variable costs (i.e. the CM), and then divide by the sales. Fixed costs divided by the contribution margin ratio will result in the dollar amount that is needed to breakeven.

Thus the formulas for these areas would be as follows:

Total Sales   Sales per Unit
-Total Variable Costs   -Variable Cost per Unit
Overall Contribution Margin   Contribution Margin per Unit

Fixed Costs / Contribution Margin per Unit = Break-even per Unit
Fixed Costs / Overall Contribution Margin = Break-even in Dollars

Again, the information that is obtained can assist managers in estimating their overall profit, for any given activity level. Since all budgeting should begin with sales, one obviously needs to know how many units it will take to breakeven. Everything above this amount will result in additional profit that may then be utilized to grow the company and reward employees.

Operating Leverage

Another useful tool is operating leverage. Operating leverage will allow a manager to determine for each percentage change in sales, how that percentage change will affect operating profit. The formula for calculating operating leverage is the contribution margin divided by operating profit. Most students do not distinguish a difference between operating profit and net income, as many textbooks teach these are essentially the same thing. Depending on the company, this is not always the case. Therefore, any amounts on exams will be clearly identified.

Decision Making

Utilizing CVP analysis for decision making allows managers to investigate different scenarios and alternatives. It is through the evaluation of the alternatives that managers can then make better informed decisions. Decisions can range from closing a division or location to determining the correct product mix. In each case, the decision will be a better one, if the manager is informed, with accurate data.

Application

One of the key concepts to decision making is reliance upon relevant information. It is what one does with that information that can potentially change the direction of a company. In a similar manner, the Bible contains all of the relevant information that one needs in order to be successful in both this life, and the life to come. When the truths contained within the Bible are revealed, the time in which it is recieved is different for each person. For some, the revelation comes earlier in life; for others, much later. What one does, once that truth has been revealed, is similar to what a manager does once they know the best route to take for the business, based on the relevant information presented. Consider Noah. He was not provided with a detailed balance sheet or income statement for the cost of building the ark. Yet, he was given all of the relevant information from God that allowed him to choose to build the ark. The benefits of following God's plan were not readily apparent; yet, the end rewards proved to justify the expense.

Now consider one's own life. Are there any parallels to Noah's story and yours? Explain.

_____

_____

_____

_____

_____

_____

James 4: 13-17 discusses business and the pursuit of profits. Companies are obviously extremely concerned with profits, so from a biblical perspective, how can CVP analysis help?

_____

_____

_____

_____

_____

_____

NOTES

MODULE

6

Module 6: Chapter 4

Job Costing

Job costing is the ability to account for those activities that result in the manufacturing of a unique custom order product. Generally, job costing is done for those items that are not mass produced, and is often considered one of the easier methods of accounting for costs. Some prime examples of products that would use job costing would include a custom built home, a specific advertising campaign, or even a movie.

The costs are accounted for through the utilization of a job costing sheet, which contains information on direct materials, direct labor, and an allocation of overhead. In effect, all costs that are directly attributable to the product are accounted for on this ticket, or in a specific chart of account. Any indirect items will be allocated to factory overhead and then allocated to the job based on a predetermined overhead rate. The formula is the estimated total factory overhead for the year, divided by the estimated total amount of the cost driver for the same time period. The predetermined overhead rate is generally based off of direct labor hours; however, if a better measurement figure is available, that figure should be utilized. The use of the estimation is then allocated to the work in process account.

Once a job is complete, the actual indirect amount may be determined. If the actual amount is different from what was estimated, then one will have either an over-applied or under-applied amount of factory overhead, which must then be allocated to either goods in process, cost of goods sold, or finished goods inventory. The account will be dependent on whether the item has been completed, whether it is still in inventory, or whether it has been sold.

Application

While this was a relatively short chapter, it does present important concepts to the area of decision making. The building of the temple has been used several times within the text to describe how one would account for costs. Are there any other examples from the Bible that show how important accurately accounting for costs can be?

_____

_____

_____

_____

_____

_____

_____

This chapter discusses the ability to estimate costs. Ideally, those estimates are fairly accurate, and are only in need of moderate changes once the actual costs are known. If one knows the measurement is not accurate; yet, they will be rewarded for having actual costs lower than what was estimated, what should that person do, from a biblical perspective?

_____

_____

_____

_____

_____

_____

NOTES

MODULE

7

Module 7: Chapter 11

Decision Making

Throughout this text, the main emphasis has been on decision making. How one makes good decisions in part depends on the type of information that is given in order to make those decisions. If the information a manager has is poor, then the likelihood that the resulting decision will be poor is high. Therefore, one must consider a variety of items in the decision making process; all of which relies on the type of decision needing to be made.

Special Orders

Special orders are those requests for products that are outside of the normal operating activities. Special considerations must be made with special orders, particularly if a company is operating at or near full capacity. Generally, special orders will require a manager to consider the opportunity cost of completing the special order in comparison to the fulfilling of the normal requests. If a company is not operating at full capacity, then the decision is much easier to make. However, if the company is operating at full capacity, and a special order comes in, then the manager must choose between their normal operations and the special order. In order to do this, the relevant costs must be examined. To examine the relevant costs, the manager will need to examine the sales level, the variable costs, and the fixed costs at two levels. The first level analyzed should be when production does not stop for the special order, but rather, continues as if nothing has happened. Once the profits for this scenario are determined, then, the manager should examine the profits with the special order, keeping in mind the amount of lost sales. The difference between the two levels will determine if the manager should accept the special order (i.e. if the amount of income generated is more with the special order in comparison to not fulfilling the special order).

Other Decisions

Other decisions that managers must also make include the make, lease, or buy decision, as well as the further processing decision. Similar to the special order decision, managers must determine the amount of profits that are earned under each of the three scenarios. The alternative that offers the best profit, and that makes sense to the company as a whole, will generally be the best decision.

Sometimes a company has the ability to produce a product that can easily be sold. With some additional costs, the company could then convert this product into an entirely different product. The question then becomes which product is the best product to produce. Consequently, the manager must first decide if there is a constraint on the availability of the product. If one cannot obtain the materials necessary, then it will obviously become increasingly difficult to make and sell the product.

Keep in mind that there are times, even when there are not materials constraints, that it is best to not process an item further. If one can make more money, more fully utilize their production facility, and in turn have a greater overall net income for the company; then, it is a decision that should be considered and not taken lightly. In each situation, the costing techniques that are utilized come from a process costing application, as opposed to a job order application. Thus, it becomes necessary to ensure that one's costs are accurate, and that only the relevant costs are being considered.

Application

The Bible is replete of examples where we, as humans, have failed. Whether it is financial decisions or personal decisions, there is a process to one's decision making. Provide one example where someone in the Bible made a wise financial decision and one example where they did not.

_____

_____

_____

_____

_____

Now consider your employer and recent business decisions. Did your employer make wise decisions, based on what has been learned in this course? Why or why not?

_____

_____

_____

_____

_____

NOTES

MODULE

8

Chapters 13 & 18

Module 8: Chapters 13 & 18

Accounting for Decision Making

Strategy is essential in any business, and most would probably state that it is essential if that business wants to succeed. Consider what has been presented, however. There is good strategy that considers relevant costs, performs analysis, and takes the time to properly budget and plan; but, there is bad strategy as well. Bad strategy is therefore not properly budgeting, planning, analyzing relevant costs, and/or not making decisions based on the information that is available. Consequently, it could be argued that good strategy is essential for the success of a company.

One consideration managers must examine is the stage of the life cycle a particular product is in. The reason this is important is because the various stages require different actions on the part of the manager, and therefore the company, in order to accurately market the product. For instance, if a product is entering the maturity stage of the life cycle, then a company is more likely to price their product relative to the competition. Whereas, if the product is new and in the introduction phase, the price of the product will be relatively low in order to promote the product, and potentially gain market share.

Another consideration is the use of target costing. Once the breakeven point is known, a manager can then use target costing to determine the number of items the company needs to sell at various sales prices in order to not only breakeven, but also maximize the market. For instance, assume a product has a total cost of $25. It is possible that one could sell one unit at $100, and therefore make a CM of $75. If, however, one were to lower the price to $60 per unit, providing a CM of $35, there is the possibility of being able to sell four units, for a total CM of $140, compared to the previous $75. Assuming all other items and costs being equal, it would be wiser for the company to lower their price, and sell more of the product; thereby earning a greater CM. Of course, there is a great deal more involved in these types of situations, but one should be able to see how changing the sales price, while temporarily limiting the CM, in the long-run could actually produce a greater CM. Consequently, the target cost is essentially what the company needs to attempt to sell the product at for the desired level of profit. It does not mean that they will get this target price, due to market demands; however, if the proper market analysis is done, management should feel fairly confident in their plan.

Cost and profit centers are at the core of a business. There are areas within the company that either drain the company of financial resources, or supplies financial resources. There are times when a particular area could operate in both manners; however, it will be depend largely on the industry and how the company is managed. Ideally, management's desire should be to turn normally operating cost centers into profit centers. This is not an easy task, and in some instances, may not be possible. The goal of the manager of a cost center should be to provide the services or costs at not only the best price possible, but to do so in such a way that the customer feels additional value has been added. Value added activities will enable a company to further differentiate itself, and possibly turn a cost center into one that is more profitable.

By knowing one's market, as well as the stage of the products that are being sold, a manager will be in a better position to maximize company profits. Through the analysis of the company's critical success factors in a balanced scorecard, a proper SWOT analysis, and the corresponding linkage between the balanced scorecard and the SWOT analysis, a company should be able to gain a competitive advantage. It is through this advantage, and the use of other management techniques previously discussed in the text, that a company will be able to make strategic decisions that not only benefit the company, but places the company in the position of the market leader, and the benchmark for all others within the industry.

Application

One's decisions often do not affect just oneself. Often times, decisions may have a profound effect on everyone around. In Proverbs 3:7, the Bible instructs, "Don't be impressed with your own wisdom..." Strategic planning requires more than just one's own wisdom. The use of wise counsel can not only assist a manager in making the proper decisions, but those decisions can have a profound impact on the company. Therefore, if one wants to seek wise Godly counsel in a business setting, what would be the best way to do so, and who would one seek the counsel from?

_____

_____

_____

_____

_____

_____

Based on everything that has been discussed within the text, there is a strong correlation between the basic strategic accounting concepts and the Bible. List two passages and describe the correlation between the passages and the concepts within the text.

_____

_____

_____

_____

_____

_____

NOTES

ADDITIONAL TOPICS

Additional Topics

Introduction

The below topics strongly correlate with the previously covered topics, and may have briefly been mentioned; however, these are areas that require repeating. The actual analysis of these topics can be quite confusing to those that do not have a strong accounting background, or for those that may not have to specifically deal with these topics in their professional life. Therefore, to ensure that the topics are covered, they are mentioned in this section to aid in the understanding of the decision making process.

Margin of Safety

Margin of safety is a consideration for many managers with regards to inventory. The purpose of margin of safety is to inform the manager how many units or dollars the firm can lose before reaching the breakeven point. Margin of safety does not tell one if they will breakeven, as the actual number of units or dollar amount is above the breakeven mark. It does however provide the manager with a safety net, as it will alert the manager that inventory is beginning to get low. If the margin of safety is reached, then managers only have a limited amount of time to correct their path before actually hitting breakeven, or worse yet, falling below breakeven. Margin of safety is not utilized to determine if a company will breakeven, as that is the purpose of breakeven. Rather, the margin of safety, though closely related to breakeven, indicates how much revenue can be lost prior to falling below the breakeven point.

Special Orders

Most individuals have a difficult time saying no to someone, particularly if it is a friend or loved one. These same people operate as managers within companies, and as a result, there are times when it is difficult to tell a customer no. Often, companies will request special orders from their main vendor. It is therefore essential for the vendor to realize that if one is operating at full or close to full capacity, the ability to complete a special order could result in opportunity cost. The opportunity cost will be the amount that is being given up in order to do the special order. Thus, one's regular production could be lost due to the special order. There are times when the special order will allow the company to actually increase the overall sales. Therefore, a determination to complete the special order should not be taken lightly.

Analysis

Finally, there is a great deal of analysis that must be done when making decisions. The numbers are extremely important; however, hopefully it has been conveyed that what underlies those numbers are equally, if not more so, important. A decision based solely on numbers would not be a wise decision. Similarly, decisions without reviewing the numbers would not be wise either. There is often more to a decision than what is on the surface. It is therefore important for managers to understand the process, the people within that process, and the ultimate goal. Utilization of resources, management techniques, and the ability to understand how everything works together becomes a strategy that should lead companies in a continuous pursuit of excellence, as opposed to a pursuit of complacency. Constant examination to find those areas that are not working, making the necessary changes, and continuously monitoring the goals, strategy, and critical success factors can become a winning combination for a company to gain a competitive edge in the global marketplace.

NOTES

FINAL CORRELATION

This section contributed by

Scott Hicks, M.B.A.

Final Correlation

The story of the Good Samaritan, found in Luke 10:30-37, is more than just a compelling story. The parable portrays human life and behavior in its simplest form. Through the examination of those within the parable, one can better understand human nature and how that nature affects business.

The first two persons introduced in the parable are that of the Jewish man and the thief. The Jewish man was quite wealthy, yet it was because of what he had been given (i.e. his wealth) that he found himself in the predicament of being beaten, almost to the point of death. The Jewish man went from essentially relying on himself to needing the assistance of others, just to survive.

In contrast, the thief was one who saw the wealth of the Jewish man and felt he deserved what the Jewish man had, despite not having earned it. The thief believed that "what's mine is mine", and "what's yours is mine, if I can get it." Therefore the thief took whatever he could from the Jewish man, and proceeded on his way, seemingly unaffected by his actions, and dependent on gaining from others (Covey, 1989; Personal communication, John George, April 1997).

The next two persons introduced were that of the priest and the Levite. Both the priest and the Levite saw the Jewish man who had been beaten severely, yet both looked away and kept traveling. Now, keep in mind that this particular road contained areas where thieves would hide and/or devise traps for unsuspecting travelers. This very easily could have been a trap; yet, both the priest and the Levite chose not to take the risk, and instead continued on their way. There are many reasons as to why they may not have stopped; it could have been close to the Sabbath, and they did not want to become unclean by being with someone who had passed away, or it could have been something as simple as they may not have wanted to get involved. It is further important to understand that both the priest and the Levite were viewed with the utmost respect in society. They were those who could make a difference, and yet chose not to do so. So often in society, Christians do not want to become involved in other's conflicts. The theory becomes one of independence "what's mine is mine, and what's yours is yours, if you can keep it" (Covey, 1989; Personal communication, John George, April 1997).

The final person that is introduced in the parable is that of the Samaritan. Remember, during this period of time in history, Samaritans were not thought too highly of, even if they were wealthy. Samaritans were thought to be unclean, and in essence a lower class human being compared to those of Jewish descent. Despite this, the Samaritan took a risk by getting off of his beast to tend to the Jewish man. Upon seeing that it was not a trap, the Samaritan felt compassion for this Jewish man, and at his own expense, cleaned his wounds, found a place for him to stay where he would be fed and housed at no expense to the

Jewish man, and genuinely showed the Jewish man, his supposed enemy, love and compassion. In essence, the Samaritan portrayed interdependence, and was telling the Jewish man that "what's yours is yours, and what's mine is yours if you need it" (Covey, 1989; Personal communication, John George, April 1997). The Samaritan showed the utmost of compassion and selfless love that one, in his sinful humanity, could bestow upon his enemy. It was an act of showing praise, glory, and thankfulness for all that God had bestowed upon him, and in return, he became dependent upon the sovereign God to provide him with all of his needs.

In today's world, particularly in the business world, there seems to be many that fall into either the category of the thief, or the category of the priest and the Levite. It is in the sinful nature that often causes the selfishness of the thief to rear its ugly head, and cause those in the world, even Christians, to act like anything but the children of God. So too, the desire and fear of the unknown, and therefore the false idea that someone will take something away that one has worked so hard to achieve, may cause some to behave similar to the priest and the Levite. One is therefore in no better shape than the one who acts like the thief or the priest and the Levite.

Understanding the character of each person in the parable can bring invaluable insight to the business world. Knowing how one will react to a given situation, and understanding what the customer desires, will eventually allow a manager to gain a deeper understanding of humanity, and in turn provide a foundation not only for oneself, but also for the strategic policies of the company in which he works. As Stephen Covey has stated in his *The Seven Habits of Highly Effective People,* one should first seek to understand, then to be understood.

Understanding the principles God has, and his desires for us, is our true North. It is through our service to Christ that others will receive the reciprocal value of that service, because He more than meets the needs and desires of man. The understanding of human nature works in concert as a co-producer (Fitzsimmons & Fitzsimmons, 2008) in providing the service to both the internal and external customers at each and every level (Personal communication, John George, April 1997). Remembering that one is unworthy of the grace and love bestowed upon us by our Heavenly Father, and sharing that grace and love, via our actions, particularly in the business world, will within the context of a business setting, provide a foundation of strategy that will benefit the internal and external customer, and more importantly allow praise and honor to be given unto God (Revelation 7:12).

As you ponder the parable of the Good Samaritan, which person are you more like? What actions will you take to become the person God has called you to be?

_____

_____

_____

_____

_____

_____

References

Covey, S. (1989). *The seven habits of highly effective people: Powerful lessons in personal change.* New York, NY: Simon & Schuster.

Fitzsimmons, J. & Fitzsimmons, M. (2008). *Service management: Operations, strategy, information technology* (6th ed.). Boston, MA: McGraw-Hill.

INDEX